Houghton
Mifflin
Harcourt

W9-ALX-506

Getting Ready for the
PARCC® Assessment

INCLUDES

- Common Core Standards Practice in PARCC® format
- Beginning-, Middle-, and End-of-Year Benchmark Tests with Performance Tasks
- Year-End Performance Assessment Task

Contents

Contents

Common Core Assessment Formats

Common Core Assessment consortia have developed assessments that contain item types beyond the traditional multiple-choice format, which allows for a more robust assessment of children's understanding of concepts.

Common Core assessments will be administered via computers; and *Getting Ready for the PARCC® Assessment* presents items in formats similar to what you will see on the tests. The following information is provided to help familiarize you with these different types of items. Each item type is identified on pages (vii–viii). The examples will introduce you to the item types.

The following explanations are provided to guide you in answering the questions. These pages (v–vi) describe the most common item types. You may find other types on some tests.

Example 1 Choose numbers less than a given number.

More Than One Correct Choice

This type of item looks like a traditional multiple-choice item, but it asks you to choose all of something. When the item asks you to find all, look for more than one correct choice. Carefully look at each choice and mark it if it is a correct answer.

Example 2 Choose tens and ones to describe a number.

Choose From a List

Sometimes when you take a test on a computer, you will have to select a word, number, or symbol from a drop-down list. The *Getting Ready for the PARCC® Assessment* tests show a list and ask you to choose the correct answer. Make your choice by circling the correct answer. There will only be one choice that is correct.

Example 3 Sort numbers into groups for greater than or less than a given number.

Sorting

You may be asked to sort something into categories. These items will present numbers, words, or equations on rectangular "tiles." The directions will ask you to write each of the items in the box that tells about it.

Sometimes you may write the same number or word in more than one box. For example, if you need to sort quadrilaterals by category, a square could be in a box labeled rectangle and another box labeled rhombus.

Example 4 Order numbers from least to greatest.

Use Given Numbers in the Answer

You may also see numbers and symbols on tiles when you are asked to write an equation or answer a question using only numbers. You should use the given numbers to write the answer to the problem. Sometimes there will be extra numbers. You may also need to use each number more than once.

Example 5 Match related facts.

Matching

Some items will ask you to match equivalent values or other related items. The directions will specify what you should match. There will be dots to guide you in drawing lines. The matching may be between columns or rows.

Item Types:

Example 1

More Than One Correct Choice

Fill in the bubble next to all the correct answers.

Choose all the numbers less than 25.

○ 32

○ 24

○ 52

○ 17

○ 61

Example 2

Choose From a List

Circle the words.

What is another way to write 24?

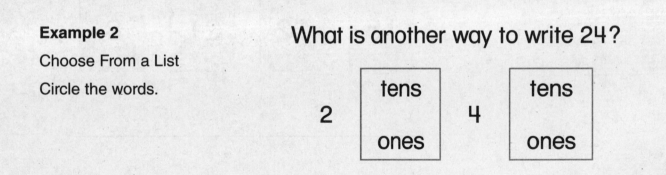

Common Core Assessment Formats

Example 3

Sorting

Copy the numbers in the right box.

Write each number in the box that tells about it.

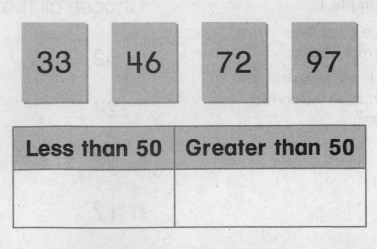

Less than 50	Greater than 50

Example 4

Use the Numbers

Write the numbers.

Write the numbers in order from least to greatest.

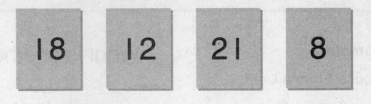

_____

Example 5

Matching

Draw lines to match.

Match the related facts.

$3 + 2 = 5$ •   • $9 - 6 = 3$

$8 - 2 = 6$ •   • $2 + 3 = 5$

$3 + 6 = 9$ •   • $2 + 7 = 9$

$9 - 7 = 2$ •   • $8 - 6 = 2$

Common Core Assessment Formats

1. Write the addition problem.

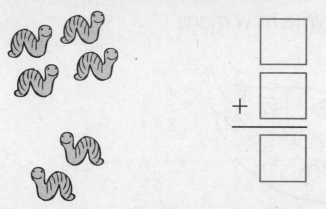

$$+$$

---

2. There are 4 red leaves and 4 yellow leaves.
How many leaves are there?

Draw to show your work.

| Write the number sentence and how many.

_____ ◯ _____ ◯ _____

---

3. James has 5 marbles. He finds more marbles.
Then he has 9 marbles. How many marbles
does James find?

$$5 + \underline{\hspace{1cm}} = 9$$

Practice Test

Name _____

4. Circle the part you are taking from the group. Then cross it out. Write how many there are now.

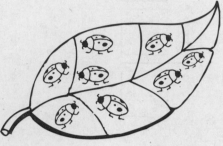

8 bugs   3 bugs walk away.   _____ bugs now

---

5. Read the problem. Use the model to solve. Complete the model and the number sentence.

There are 8 cows in a barn. 2 cows are brown. The others are white. How many cows are white?

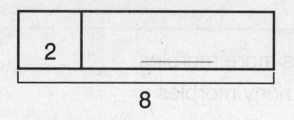

$8 - 2 =$ _____

---

6. Jake has 13 pencils. He gives some away. He has 8 left. How many pencils does he give away? Draw or write to explain.

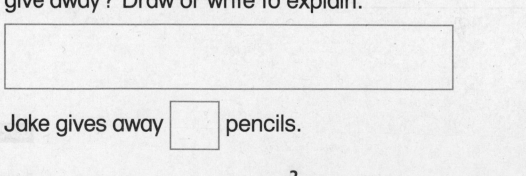

Jake gives away ▢ pencils.

1. Ted has 7 red apples. He has 3 yellow apples. He has 2 green apples. Draw a picture of the apples.

Ted has ☐ apples.

2. Jude has 8 green blocks, 4 red blocks, and 2 green blocks. How many blocks does Jude have?

☐ _____
   label

3. Paula has 6 red flowers. She has 4 pink flowers. She has 7 yellow flowers. Draw a picture of the flowers.

Paula has ☐ flowers.

Name _____

4. Beth sees 4 red birds. She sees 2 yellow birds. She sees 4 blue birds. Draw a picture of the birds.

Beth sees [   ] birds.

Circle the number that makes the sentence true.

5. David has 6 red markers, 5 green markers, and 7 blue markers. How many markers does David have in all?

David has | 11 / 12 / 18 | markers.

6. Enzo has 5 blue pens. He has 4 green pens. He has 5 red pens. Draw a picture of the pens.

Enzo has [   ] pens.

4

STOP

Practice Test

1.OA.B.3
Understand and apply properties of operations and the relationship between addition and subtraction.

1. Choose all the pictures that show adding zero.

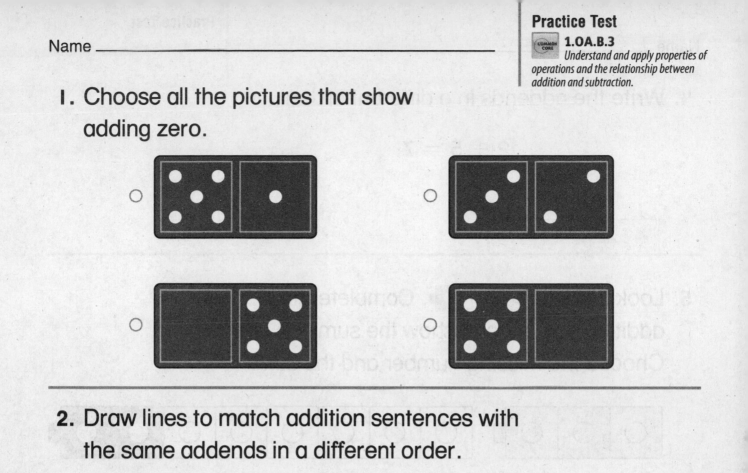

2. Draw lines to match addition sentences with the same addends in a different order.

$4 + 3 = 7$ $2 + 4 = 6$ $3 + 6 = 9$

$4 + 2 = 6$ $6 + 3 = 9$ $3 + 4 = 7$

3. Draw a model to show that $5 + 3$ is the same as $3 + 5$. Show how you know.

GO ON

Name _____

4. Write the addends in a different order.

$$2 + 5 = 7$$

_____ + _____ = 7

5. Look at the 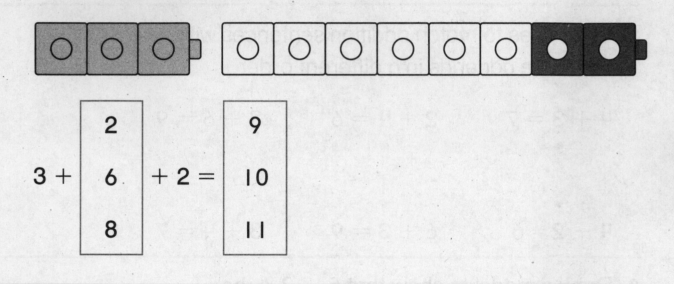. Complete the
addition sentence to show the sum.
Choose the missing number and the sum.

$$3 + \begin{array}{|c|} \hline 2 \\ 6 \\ 8 \\ \hline \end{array} + 2 = \begin{array}{|c|} \hline 9 \\ 10 \\ 11 \\ \hline \end{array}$$

6. Write two ways to group and add 3 + 6 + 1.

_____ + _____ = _____

_____ + _____ = _____

Practice Test

COMMON CORE **1.OA.B.4**
Understand and apply properties of operations and the relationship between addition and subtraction.

1. Look at the facts. A number is missing.
Which number is missing?

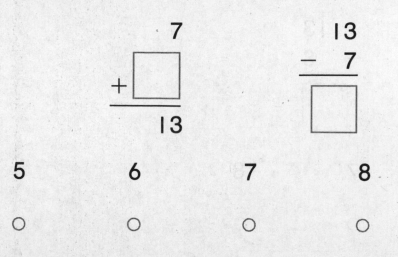

5	6	7	8
○	○	○	○

2. Write a subtraction sentence you can solve by using $4 + 2 = 6$.

$$\boxed{} - \boxed{} = \boxed{}$$

3. Look at the facts.
Write the missing number in each fact.

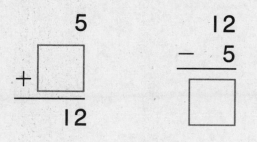

GO ON

Practice Test

Name _____

4. Look at the facts. A number is missing.
Which number is missing?

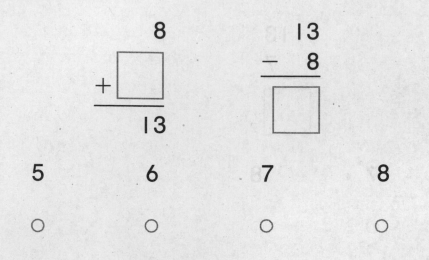

$$8$$
$$+ \boxed{}$$
$$\overline{13}$$

$$13$$
$$- 8$$
$$\boxed{}$$

5   6   7   8

○   ○   ○   ○

---

5. Write a subtraction sentence you can
solve by using $5 + 4 = 9$.

$$\boxed{} - \boxed{} = \boxed{}$$

---

6. Write a subtraction sentence
you can solve by using $3 + 9 = 12$.

_____ − _____ = _____

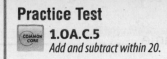

1. Count on from 6. Write the number that shows 2 more.

_____

2. Count back. Write the number that is 1 less.

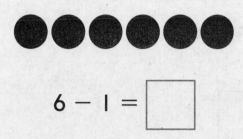

$$6 - 1 = \boxed{}$$

3. ☆ means "count back 1."

⬜ means "count back 2."

⚫ means "count back 3."

Match each picture to a number sentence.

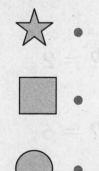

• $8 - ? = 6$

• $6 - ? = 3$

• $11 - ? = 10$

4. Count on from 4. Write the number that shows 1 more.

_____

5. Count back. Write the number that is 2 less.

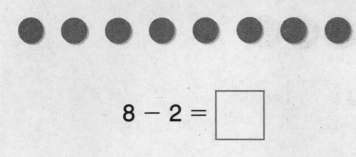

$$8 - 2 = \boxed{}$$

6. ☆ means "count back 1."

⬛ means "count back 2."

⬤ means "count back 3."

Match each picture to a number sentence.

1. Write the subtraction sentence the picture shows.

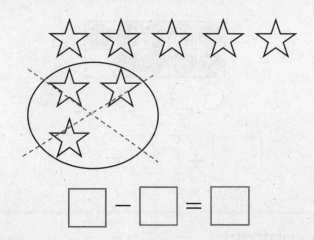

☐ − ☐ = ☐

Explain.

_____

_____

_____

2. Write a count on 2 fact to show a sum of 6. Then write a doubles fact to show a sum of 6.

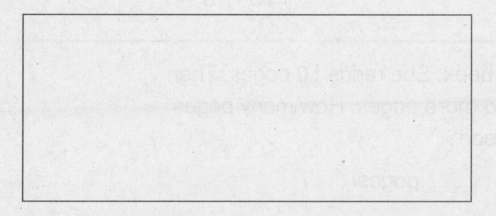

© Houghton Mifflin Harcourt Publishing Company

Name _____

3. The model shows $9 + 2 = 11$. Write the 10 fact that has the same sum.

[ ] + [ ] = [ ]

---

4. Make a ten to subtract. Draw to show your work. Write the difference.

$15 - 8 = \boxed{?}$

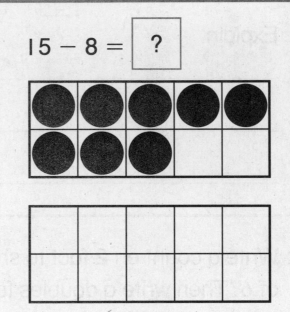

$15 - 8 = \boxed{}$

---

5. Tina has a book. She reads 10 pages. Then she reads 6 more pages. How many pages does she read?

Tina reads _____ pages.

Write a related fact to check.

_____ − _____ = 10

Practice Test

COMMON CORE **1.OA.D.7**
Work with addition and subtraction equations.

Which are true? Circle your answers.
Which are false? Cross out your answers.

1. $1 + 9 = 9 - 1$ | $8 + 1 = 2 + 7$ | $19 = 19$

2. $8 = 5 + 3$ | $8 + 5 = 5 + 8$ | $6 + 2 = 4 + 4$

3. $9 + 7 = 16$ | $16 - 9 = 9 + 7$ | $9 - 7 = 7 + 9$

4. $12 - 3 = 9 - 0$ | $11 = 1 + 5 + 5$ | $10 = 8 - 2$

5. Which is true?

○ $5 - 4 = 9 - 8$

○ $13 = 5 + 7$

○ $6 + 2 = 2 + 8$

GO ON

Name _____

6. Choose all the math sentences that are true.

○ 6 + 3 = 3 + 6

○ 10 = 6 + 4

○ 5 + 2 = 4 − 3

7. Which are true? Use a ✏ to color.

20 = 20	9 + 1 + 1 = 11	8 − 0 = 8
12 = 1 + 2	10 + 1 = 1 + 10	7 = 14 + 7
	6 = 2 + 2 + 2	
	11 − 5 = 1 + 5	
	1 + 2 + 3 = 4 + 5	

8. Which math sentence is true?

○ 7 + 2 = 9 − 2

○ 9 = 6 + 2

○ 5 + 4 = 4 + 5

14

1. Look at the picture. How many fewer plates are there than cups? Choose the number.

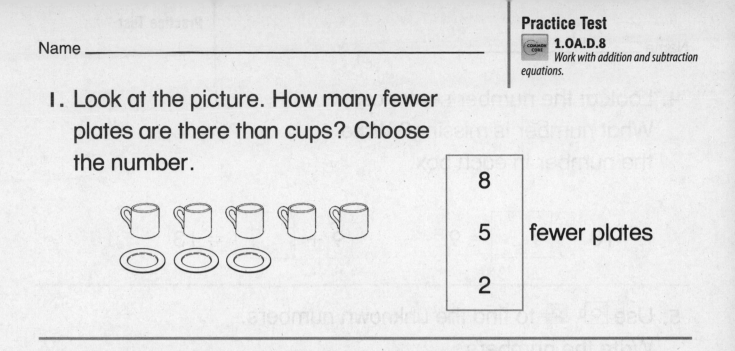

8
5	fewer plates
2

2. Use 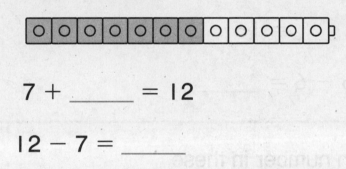 to find the unknown numbers. Write the numbers.

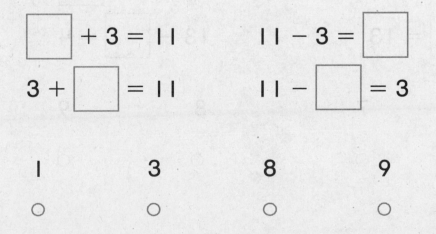

$7 +$ _____ $= 12$

$12 - 7 =$ _____

3. Which is the unknown number in these related facts?

$\boxed{} + 3 = 11$ $11 - 3 = \boxed{}$

$3 + \boxed{} = 11$ $11 - \boxed{} = 3$

   1   3   8   9

   ○   ○   ○   ○

Name _____

4. Look at the number sentences.
What number is missing? Write
the number in each box.

$$13 - \boxed{} = 9 \qquad\qquad 9 + \boxed{} = 13$$

5. Use 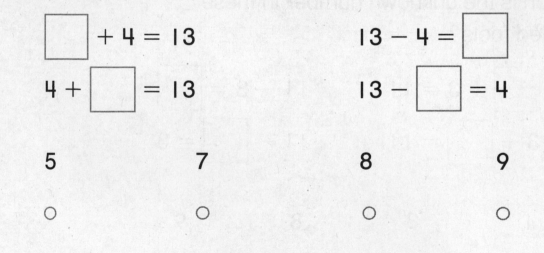, to find the unknown numbers.
Write the numbers.

$$6 + \underline{} = 16$$

$$16 - 6 = \underline{}$$

6. Which is the unknown number in these
related facts?

$$\boxed{} + 4 = 13 \qquad\qquad 13 - 4 = \boxed{}$$

$$4 + \boxed{} = 13 \qquad\qquad 13 - \boxed{} = 4$$

5	7	8	9
○	○	○	○

Practice Test
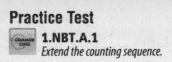
1.NBT.A.1
Extend the counting sequence.

1. Lucy counts 38 cubes. Then she counts forward some more cubes. Write the numbers.

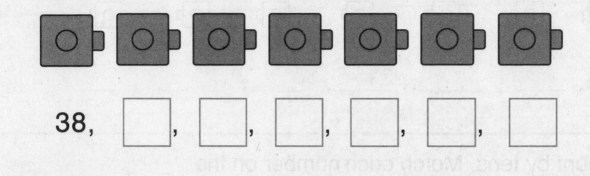

38, ☐ , ☐ , ☐ , ☐ , ☐ , ☐

2. Match each number on the left to a number that is 10 more.

29 •   • 25

45 •   • 39

69 •   • 79

15 •   • 55

3. What number does the model show?

||||||||| ooo _____

Name _____

4. Felix counts 46 cubes. Then he counts forward some more cubes. Write the numbers.

□ □ □ □ □ □ □

46, _____, _____, _____, _____, _____, _____

5. Count by tens. Match each number on the left to a number that is 10 more.

35 •   • 69

49 •   • 59

59 •   • 75

65 •   • 45

57 •   • 67

6. What number does the model show?

_____

1. Choose all the ways that name the model.

○ 70

○ 7 tens

○ 7 tens 0 ones

○ 7 ones

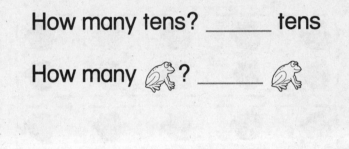

---

2. Count the 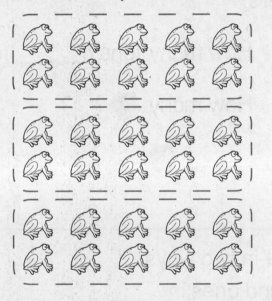. Write the numbers.

How many tens? _____ tens

How many 🐸? _____ 🐸

---

3. Draw a quick picture to show 42 in two ways.
Then write the number of tens and ones in
each picture.

```



```

____ tens ____ ones   ____ tens ____ ones

GO ON ➡

4. Choose all the ways that name the model.

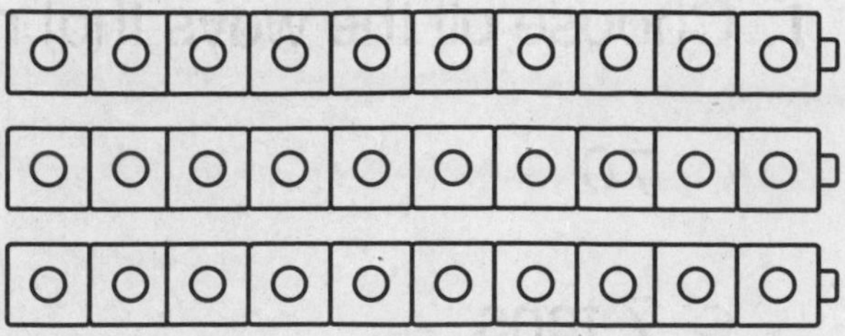

○ 3 ones

○ 3 tens

○ 3 tens 0 ones

○ 30

5. Count the 🌰. Write the numbers.

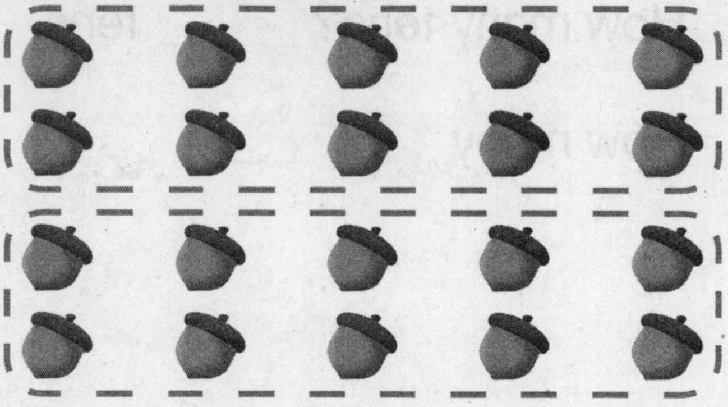

How many tens? _____ tens

How many 🌰? _____

_____ 🌰

6. Draw a quick picture to show 54 in two ways. Then write the number of tens and ones in each picture.

_____ tens _____ ones   _____ tens _____ ones

1. Which shows a number that matches the model?

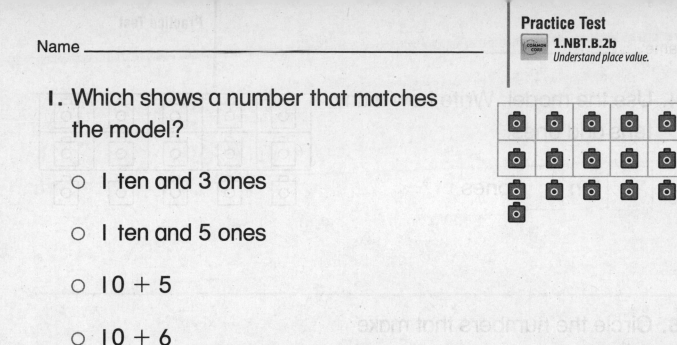

- ○ 1 ten and 3 ones

- ○ 1 ten and 5 ones

- ○ 10 + 5

- ○ 10 + 6

---

2. Circle the numbers that make the sentence true.

There are
| 10 |
| 5 |
| 1 |
tens and
| 10 |
| 5 |
| 1 |
ones in 15.

Draw 10-sticks and circles.
Write how many tens and ones.

3. 13

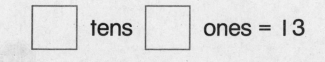

[ ] tens [ ] ones = 13

GO ON

4. Use the model. Write how many tens and ones.

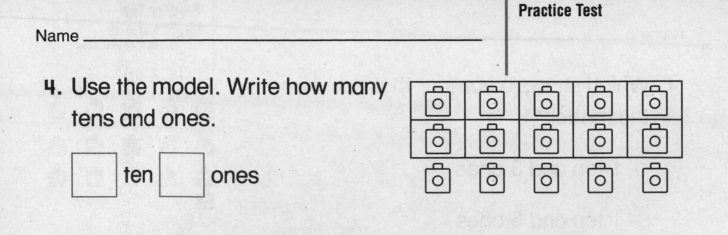

[ ] ten [ ] ones

5. Circle the numbers that make the sentence true.

There are
| 1 |
| 2 |
| 10 |
tens and
| 1 |
| 2 |
| 10 |
ones in 12.

6. How many markers?

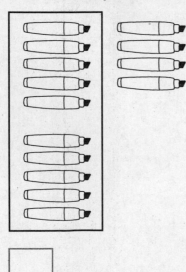

[ ]

Practice Test

1. There are 27 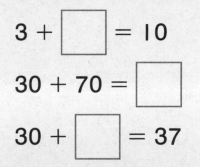. Dave says that there are
7 tens and 2 ones. Kara says there are 2 tens and 7 ones.
Who is correct? Circle the name.

Dave   Kara

How can you draw to show 27?

2. Find the unknown numbers to complete
the set of equations.

$3 + \boxed{} = 10$

$30 + 70 = \boxed{}$

$30 + \boxed{} = 37$

3. Choose all the ways that name the model.

- ○ 90

- ○ 9 tens

- ○ 9 tens 0 ones

- ○ 9 ones

GO ON

Name _____

4. There are 42 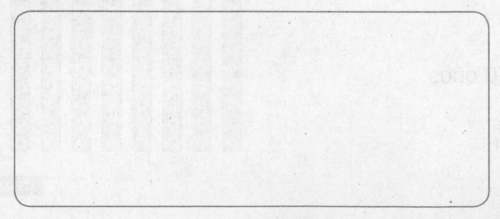. Lisa says that there are
4 tens and 2 ones. Elena says there are 2 tens
and 4 ones. Who is correct? Circle the name.

Lisa   Elena

How can you draw to show 42?

+-------------------------------------+
| |
| |
| |
+-------------------------------------+

---

5. Find the unknown numbers to complete
the set of equations.

$\boxed{} + 3 = 9$

$60 + \boxed{} = 90$

$60 + 3 = \boxed{}$

---

6. Write a number from 10 to 40.
Add 2 tens. Write the new number.
Draw and write to compare the numbers.

+-------------------------------------+
| |
| |
| |
| |
| |
+-------------------------------------+

STOP

Practice Test

1. Circle the words that make the
sentence true.

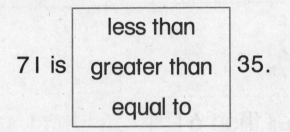

71 is | less than / greater than / equal to | 35.

---

2. Choose all the numbers that are less than 51.

○ 41

○ 48

○ 75

○ 37

---

3. Circle the symbol that makes the math
sentence true.

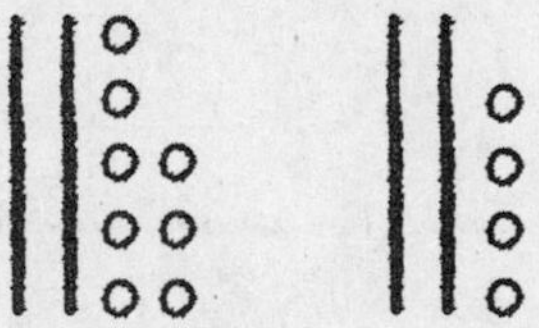

28 | > < = | 24

Practice Test

Name _____

4. Greg has these number cards. Write each number in the box to show **less than** 61 or **greater than** 61.

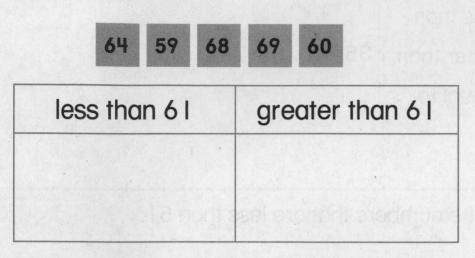

less than 61	greater than 61

---

5. Choose all the math sentences that are true.

○ 27 > 31

○ 35 = 35

○ 71 < 77

○ 82 < 70

○ 64 > 46

---

6. Write <, >, or = to compare the numbers.

46 _____ 58

26

Name ______________________________

1.NBT.C.4 *Use place value understanding and properties of operations to add and subtract.*

1. Choose all the ways that name the model.

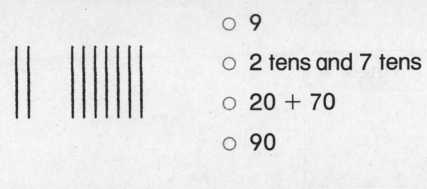

- ○ 9
- ○ 2 tens and 7 tens
- ○ 20 + 70
- ○ 90

---

2. Use the model. Draw to show how to add the ones.

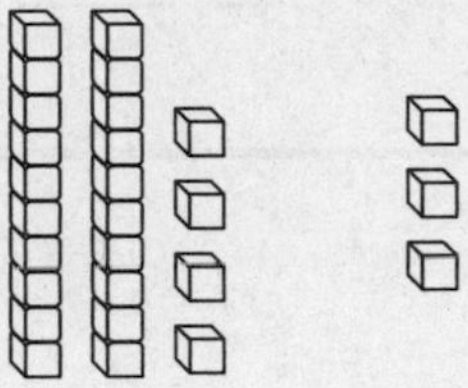

24 + 3 = ______

---

3. Use the model. Draw to show how to make a ten.

37 + 6 = ______

GO ON

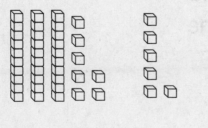

Name _____

4. Write the addition sentence that the model shows. Solve.

Tens	Ones

_____ + _____ = _____

---

5. What is the sum?

$$\begin{array}{r} 30 \\ +40 \\ \hline \end{array}$$

○ 20 ○ 70
○ 50 ○ 80

---

6. Gina has 14 pennies. Her brother gives her 23 more. How many pennies does Gina have? Circle the number that makes the sentence true.

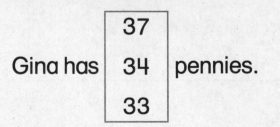

Gina has | 37 | pennies.
| 34 |
| 33 |

Name _____

Practice Test
1.NBT.C.5
Use place value understanding and
properties of operations to add and subtract.

1. Use mental math. Complete the chart.

10 Less		10 More
_____	22	_____
_____	45	_____

2. Draw a quick picture to show a number that is 10 less than the model.

3. Use mental math. Write the numbers that are 10 less and 10 more.

☐   24   ☐

Name _____

4. Use mental math. Complete the chart.

10 Less		10 More
_____	33	_____
_____	57	_____

5. Draw a quick picture to show a number that is 10 more than the model.

6. Use mental math. Write the numbers that are 10 less and 10 more.

☐   37   ☐

Name _____

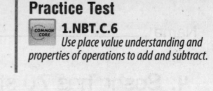
1. Bruno has 90 shirts in his store. He sells 40 of them. How many shirts are left? Show your work.

   _____ shirts

2. Match the math sentences that count up and back by tens.

   $47 + 40 = ?$ $57 + 30 = ?$ $46 + 10 = ?$

   $56 - 10 = ?$ $87 - 40 = ?$ $87 - 30 = ?$

3. Find the sum of 20 and 32. Use any way to add.

   $20 + 32 =$ _____

   Explain how you solved the problem.

GO ON

31

Name _____

4. Sasha has 70 stickers. She uses 40 of them. How many stickers are left? Show your work.

_____ stickers

---

5. Match the math sentences that count up and back by tens.

$38 + 30 = ?$ $48 + 40 = ?$ $38 + 20 = ?$

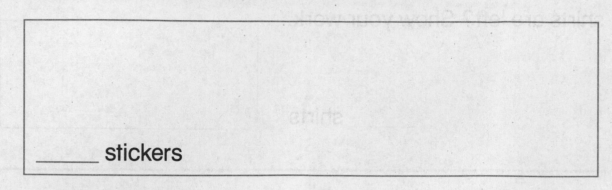

$58 - 20 = ?$ $68 - 30 = ?$ $88 - 40 = ?$

---

6. Find the sum of 62 and 15. Use any way to add.

$62 + 15 =$ _____

Explain how you solved the problem.

Practice Test

1.MD.A.1
Measure lengths indirectly and by iterating length units.

I. Match each word on the left to a drawing on the right.

shortest •

longest •

2. Which picture shows the second line shorter than the first line?

○

○

○

3. The  🖊️ is longer than the 🖍️. 
The 🖍️ is longer than the ～～. 
Draw the length of the ～～.

Practice Test

GO ON ➡

Name _____

4. Match each word on the left to
a drawing on the right.

shortest •

longest •

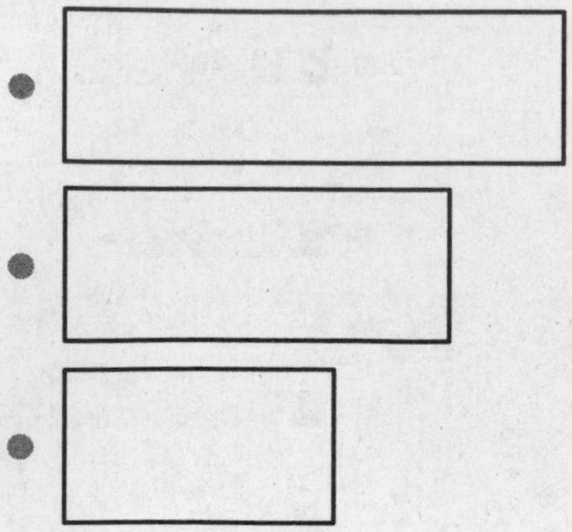

5. Which picture shows the second line shorter
than the first line?

○

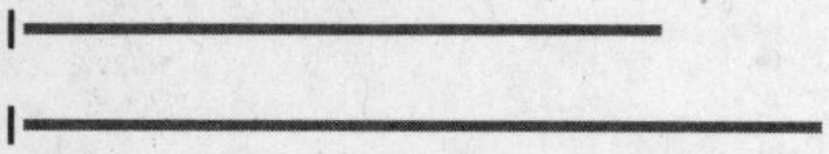

○

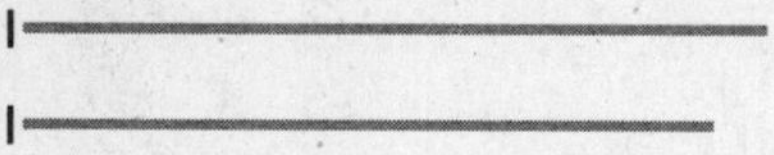

○

6. The ⟨clip⟩ is shorter than the ⟨crayon⟩.
The ⟨pencil⟩ is longer than the ⟨crayon⟩.
Draw the length of the ⟨crayon⟩.

1. The ribbon is about 3 tiles long. Draw tiles below the ribbon to show its length.

2. Measure the ▬ . Use ⬯ .

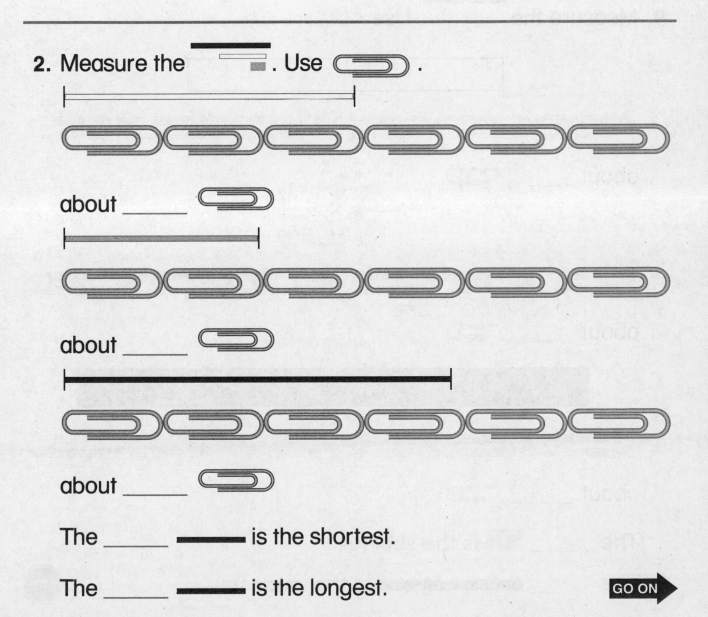

about _____ ⬯

about _____ ⬯

about _____ ⬯

The _____ ▬▬ is the shortest.

The _____ ▬▬ is the longest.

GO ON

Name _____

3. The crayon is about 5 tiles long. Draw tiles below the crayon to show its length.

4. Measure the ▭. Use ⊂⊃.

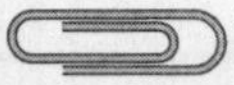

about _____ ⊂⊃

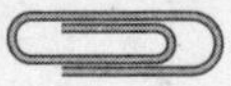

about _____ ⊂⊃

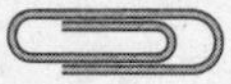

about _____ ⊂⊃

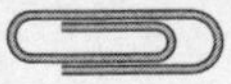

The _____ ▨ is the shortest.

The _____ ▬▬▬ is the longest.

STOP

36

Name _____

1. Look at the hour hand. What is the time?

- ○ 2:00
- ○ 3 o'clock
- ○ 4 o'clock
- ○ 5:00

---

2. What time is it? Circle the time that makes the sentence true.

The time is
2:30
3:00
3:30

---

3. Draw a hand on the clock to show 3:00.

GO ON

Name _____

4. Dan tried to show 4:00. He made a mistake.

Draw hands on the clock to show 4:00.

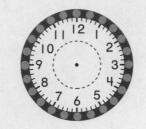

What did Dan do wrong? Explain Dan's mistake.

_____

5. Look at the hour hand. What is the time?

- ○ 9:00
- ○ 10 o'clock
- ○ 11 o'clock
- ○ 12:00

6. Draw the hand on the clock to show 9:30.

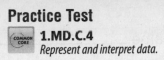

Use the picture graph to answer the questions.

Pets We Have						
🐕 dog	🧍	🧍	🧍	🧍	🧍	🧍
🐈 cat	🧍	🧍	🧍	🧍	🧍	
🐹 hamster	🧍	🧍				

Each 🧍 stands for 1 child.

1. How many children have 🐈 ?

   [ ]

2. How many more children have dogs than cats?

   [ ]

3. 1 more child gets a 🐹. Draw what the hamster row looks like now.

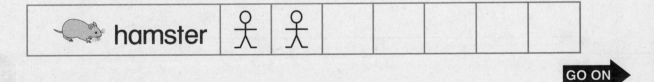

🐹 hamster	🧍	🧍				

GO ON ➡

39

Name _____

Use the bar graph to answer the questions.

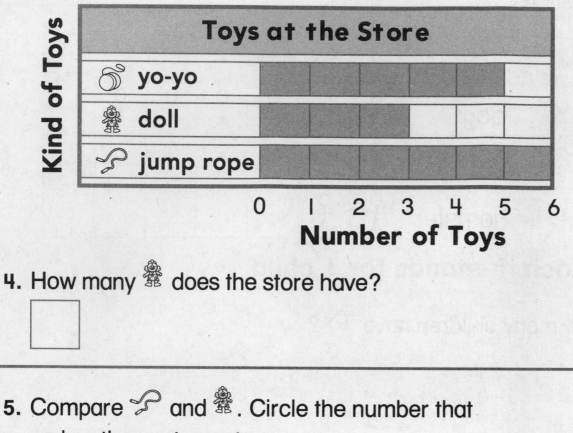

4. How many does the store have?

[ ]

---

5. Compare and . Circle the number that makes the sentence true.

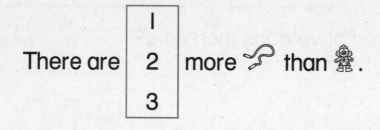

There are | 1 / 2 / 3 | more than .

---

6. Jason says the graph shows 2 more yo-yos than dolls. Is he correct? Explain your answer.

1. Match each shape to the group where it belongs.

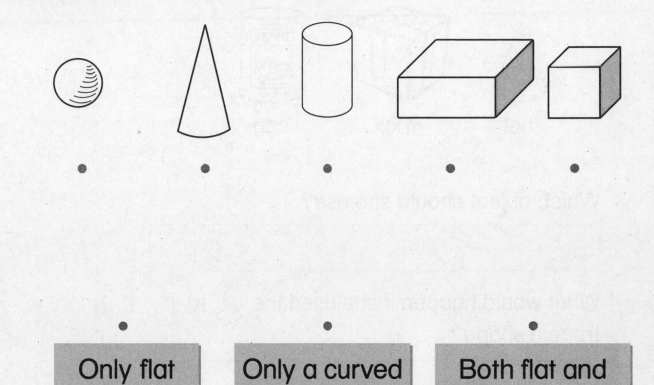

| Only flat surfaces | Only a curved surface | Both flat and curved surfaces |

2. Circle the number that makes the sentence true.

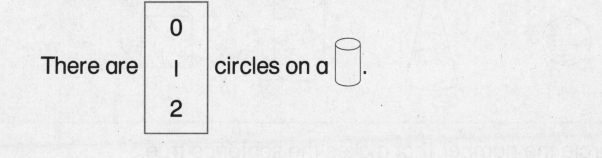

There are
0
1
2
circles on a ⬚.

Name _____

3. Adela wants to trace a . She finds these objects.

hat   box   can

Which object should she use?

_____

What would happen if she used the 🎉 to trace a shape?

_____

4. Which shape has only a curved surface?

○   ○   ○   ○

5. Circle the number that makes the sentence true.

A ⏢ has | 2 3 4 | vertices (corners).

42

Practice Test

COMMON CORE **1.G.A.2**
Reason with shapes and their attributes.

1. Combine ▢ and ▭. Choose all the new shapes you can make.

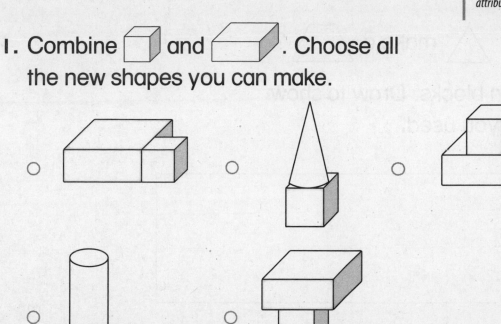

○   ○   ○

○   ○

---

2. Velma built this shape.

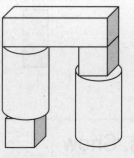

Choose all the shapes Velma used.

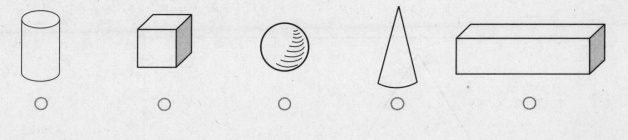

○   ○   ○   ○   ○

Name _____

3. How many  make a 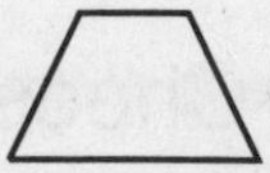 ?

Use pattern blocks. Draw to show
the blocks you used.

4. Circle two shapes that can combine to make
this new shape.

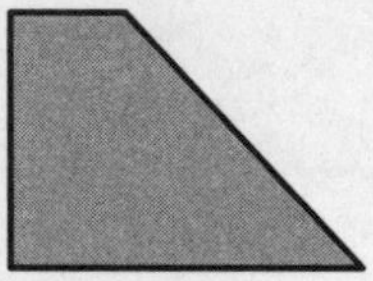

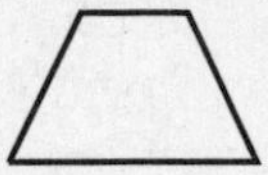

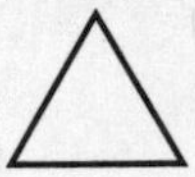

5. Draw a line to show the parts. Show
I and I .

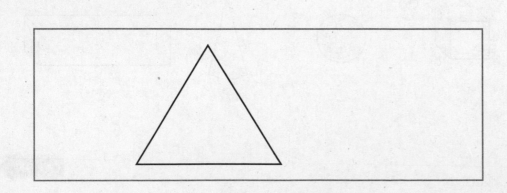

Name _____

Name _____

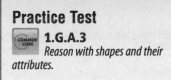
1. Choose all the shapes that show equal shares.

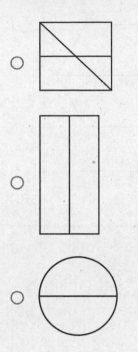

2. Choose all the shapes that show equal shares.

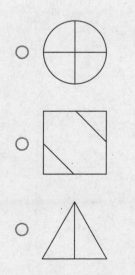

Name _____

3. Circle the shapes that show halves.

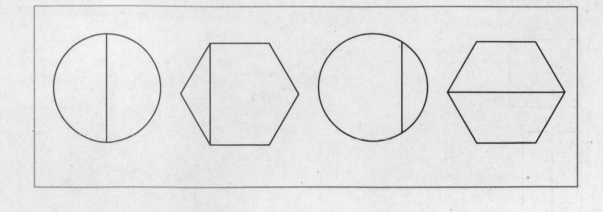

---

4. Draw lines to show fourths.

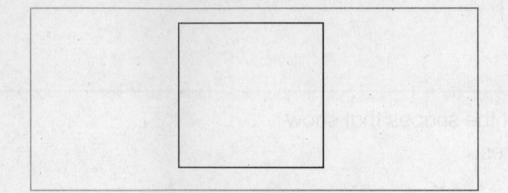

How many equal shares did you draw?

How many halves can you show
in a square?

Tell how you can solve this problem in a
different way.

1. Use the ⊂⊃ below. About how long is the marker?

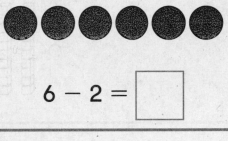

about _____ ⊂⊃

2. Count back. Write the number that is 2 less.

●●●●●●

$6 - 2 = \boxed{}$

3. José built this shape.

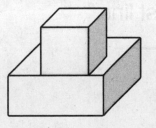

Which objects did José use? Circle them.

Draw another way to combine the objects.

GO ON ➤

47

4. Choose all the ways that show the same number.

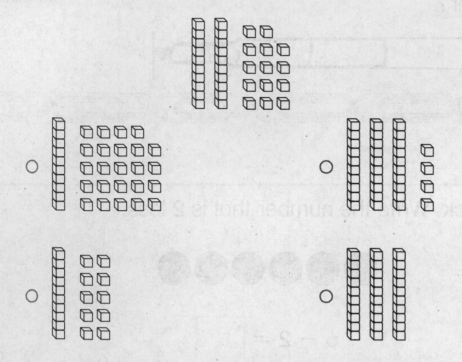

5. Choose all the pictures where the second line is shorter than the first line.

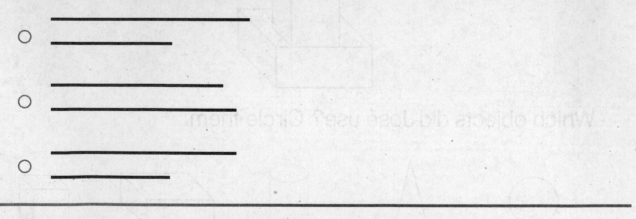

6. Use mental math. Write the numbers that are 10 less and 10 more than the number shown.

☐ 66 ☐

 GO ON

7. Look at the number sentences. What number is missing? Write the number in each box.

$$15 - \boxed{} = 9 \qquad 9 + \boxed{} = 15$$

---

8. Use the hundred chart to add.
Count on by ones or tens.

$$54 + 20 = \underline{}$$

Explain how you used the chart to find the sum.

1	2	3	4	5	6	7	8	9	10
11	12	13	14	15	16	17	18	19	20
21	22	23	24	25	26	27	28	29	30
31	32	33	34	35	36	37	38	39	40
41	42	43	44	45	46	47	48	49	50
51	52	53	54	55	56	57	58	59	60
61	62	63	64	65	66	67	68	69	70
71	72	73	74	75	76	77	78	79	80
81	82	83	84	85	86	87	88	89	90
91	92	93	94	95	96	97	98	99	100

---

9. Chet has 13 shells. He gives 6 away.
How many does he have left?

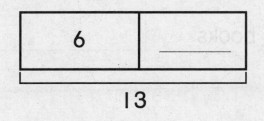

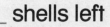

_____ shells left

10. Draw a line to show one half. Color one half of the shape.

11. Read the problem. Write a number to solve.

   I am greater than 36.
   I am less than 40.
   I have 8 ones.

12. Zeke has 60 books. He gives away 20 of them. How many books does he have now? Show your work.

   _____ books

13. Choose all the ways that name the time
on the clock.

○ 8:30   ○ 6:30

○ half past 6:00   ○ half past 8:00

---

14. Which shapes are curved? Choose all that apply.

○ ◯   ○ ▢   ○ ◯   ○ △   ○ ▭

---

15. Write each addition sentence in the box that shows the sum.

1 + 5   4 + 0   3 + 2   0 + 4   5 + 1

4	5	6

GO ON ➡

16. Look at the facts. A number is missing.
    Which number is missing?

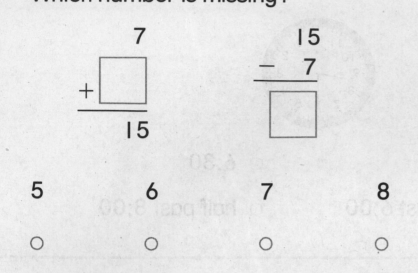

  5   6   7   8

  ○   ○   ○   ○

17. Finish the drawing to show 115.

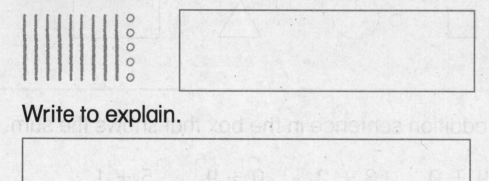

Write to explain.

18. Circle the numbers that make the sentence true.

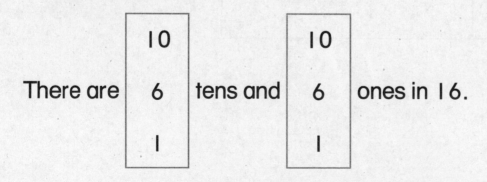

There are [10 / 6 / 1] tens and [10 / 6 / 1] ones in 16.

19. Write a number to make the sentence true.

$2 + 10 = 7 +$ ____

Use the tally chart to answer questions 20 and 21.

Our Favorite Lunch		Total
🍕 pizza		8
🥗 salad	ⅢⅢ	
🍝 spaghetti	Ⅲ	

20. How many children chose 🥗?

---

21. Circle the words that make the sentence true.

The number of
tally marks for 🥗 is

| greater than |
| less than |
| equal to |

the number of
tally marks for 🍝.

22. Circle the number that makes the sentence true.

Ava has 7 white shirts, 3 blue shirts, and 5 gray shirts. How many shirts does Ava have in all?

Ava has 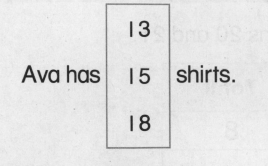 shirts.

13

15

18

---

23. Match the models to the number sentences.

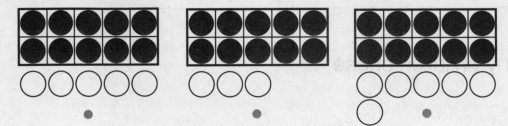

$10 + 3 = 13$ $10 + 5 = 15$ $10 + 6 = 16$

---

24. Circle the symbol that makes the math sentence true.

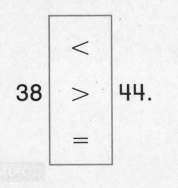

38 $<$ $>$ $=$ 44.

At the Block Party

Jason, Kwame, and Lola go to a block party. There are balloons, games, pony rides, and snacks.

**Jason gets 12 balloons.
Some are green. Some are yellow.**

1. Draw Jason's balloons. Write a number sentence about them.

2. Jason gets 3 more green balloons. How many green balloons does he have now? How many balloons does he have in all? Write number sentences to tell how you know.

_____ green balloons

_____ balloons in all

Beginning-of-Year Test

**Lola plays a game. There are 10 blocks.
Lola throws a ball to knock over some
of the blocks.**

3. Draw a picture to show the blocks.
   Cross out the ones Lola knocks over.
   Write a subtraction sentence to show
   how many blocks are left.

4. Lola knocks over the rest of the blocks
   one at a time. Write subtraction sentences
   to show how many blocks are left each time.

There are some kids waiting at the pony ride. The number of kids is more than 3 and fewer than 8.

5. Draw the kids waiting in line. Then, draw the same number of kids again to make a double.

_____

6. Write the addition sentence to show how many kids there are now.

**Kwame goes to the snack stand.
He gets 17 snacks. Some snacks
are bananas. The rest are apples.**

7. Draw pictures to show Kwame's snacks.
   Write how many bananas and apples he has.

_____ bananas   _____ apples

Write a number sentence to tell how you
know your answers are correct.

8. Write the related facts about Kwame's snacks.

1. Use the 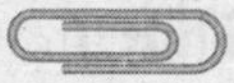 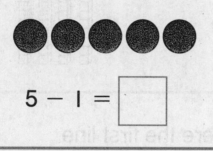 below. About how long is the ==========?

about _____ ⬭

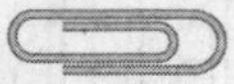

---

2. Count back. Write the number that is 1 less.

●●●●●

$5 - 1 = \boxed{}$

---

3. Ellen built this shape.

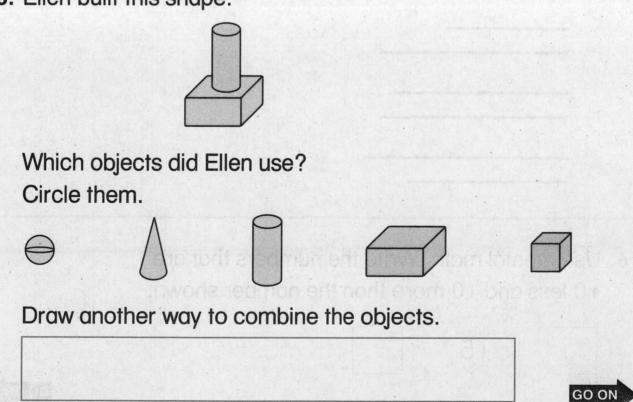

Which objects did Ellen use?
Circle them.

Draw another way to combine the objects.

GO ON ➡

59

4. Choose all the ways that show the same number.

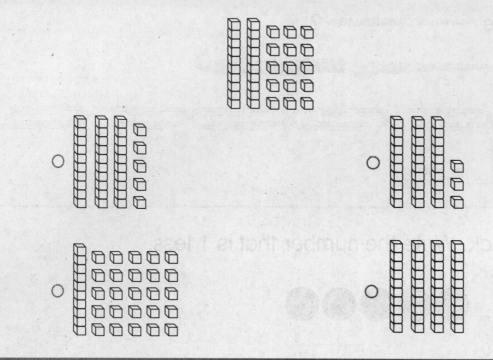

5. Choose all the pictures where the first line
is shorter than the second line.

6. Use mental math. Write the numbers that are
10 less and 10 more than the number shown.

☐   15   ☐

Middle-of-Year Test

7. Look at the number sentences.
What number is missing? Write
the number in each box.

$13 - \boxed{} = 9$ $\qquad$ $9 + \boxed{} = 13$

---

8. Use the hundred chart to add.
Count on by ones or tens.

$37 + 5 = \underline{\qquad}$

Explain how you used the
chart to find the sum.

1	2	3	4	5	6	7	8	9	10
11	12	13	14	15	16	17	18	19	20
21	22	23	24	25	26	27	28	29	30
31	32	33	34	35	36	37	38	39	40
41	42	43	44	45	46	47	48	49	50
51	52	53	54	55	56	57	58	59	60
61	62	63	64	65	66	67	68	69	70
71	72	73	74	75	76	77	78	79	80
81	82	83	84	85	86	87	88	89	90
91	92	93	94	95	96	97	98	99	100

---

9. Julia buys 12 books. She gives 9 books away.
How many books does she have left?

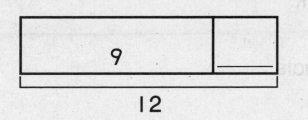

_____ books left

$\qquad$ **Middle-of-Year Test**

10. Kayla made a pie.
Color one half of the pie.

11. Read the problem. Write a number to solve.

I am greater than 27.
I am less than 30.
I have 9 ones.

12. Bette has 80 hats in her store.
She sells 30 of them. How many
hats are left? Show your work.

_____ hats

13. Choose all the ways that name the time on the clock.

○ half past 6:00   ○ half past 11:00

○ 6:00   ○ 11:30

---

14. Which shapes have only 3 sides?
Choose all that apply.

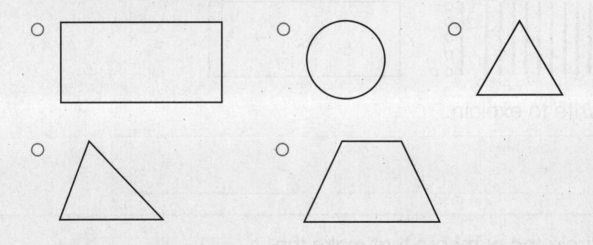

---

15. Write each addition sentence in the box that shows the sum.

$4 + 3$ $3 + 4$ $3 + 3$ $3 + 5$ $5 + 3$

6	7	8

Middle-of-Year Test

16. Look at the facts. A number is missing.
Which number is missing?

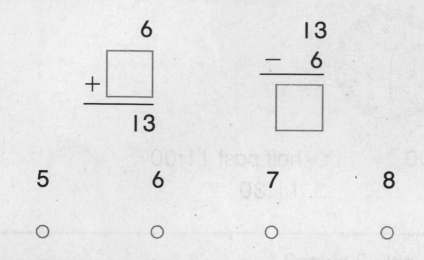

6	13
+ ☐	– 6
13	☐

5   6   7   8

○   ○   ○   ○

---

17. Finish the drawing to show 118.

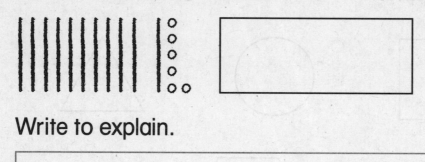

Write to explain.

---

18. Circle the numbers that make the
sentence true.

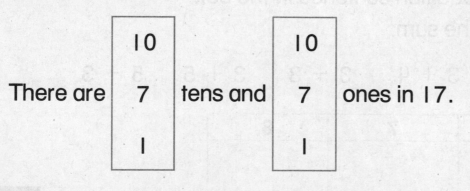

There are | 10 | tens and | 10 | ones in 17.
          | 7 | | 7 |
          | 1 | | 1 |

GO ON ➡

Middle-of-Year Test

Write a number to make the sentence true.

19. _____ = 2 + 3 + 4

_____

20. Yuki sees 3 🛻. She sees 2 more 🚗
than 🛻. She sees 1 fewer 🚐 than 🛻.
Graph the data.

What Yuki Sees						
🚗 car						
🛻 truck						
🚐 van						

0   1   2   3   4   5   6

_____

21. Use Yuki's graph to answer the question.

How many 🚗 does Yuki see?

☐

GO ON

22. Circle the number that makes the sentence true.
Boris has 8 small boxes, 2 medium boxes,
and 4 large boxes. How many boxes does
Boris have in all?

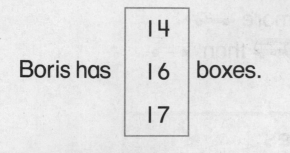

Boris has [14 / 16 / 17] boxes.

23. Match the models to the number sentences.

10 + 3 = 13   10 + 1 = 11   10 + 0 = 10

24. Eric has 57 stickers. Jeremy has 49
stickers. Jeremy says he has more stickers
than Eric. Is he correct? Explain your
answer.

Lucy's Craft Store

Lucy has a craft store.
At the store children do projects with beads,
stickers, buttons, and clay.
Today many children are in the store making
projects.

Janey makes a necklace with beads.
Beads come in packs of 10.
She needs more than 40 beads.
She needs fewer than 50 beads.

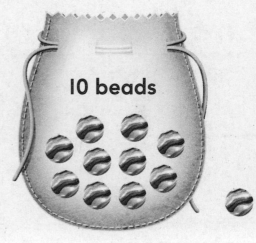

10 beads

1. Write a number of beads Janey can
use. Draw packs of beads and single
beads to show the number.
Write how many tens and ones.

2. Show the same number of beads in a
different way. Use pictures, words,
and numbers.

---

3. Janey adds another pack of 10 beads.
Write the number of beads Janey has now.

**Meg, Kira, and Juan put stickers on a
poster. Stickers come in packs of 10.
The chart shows the stickers they use.**

Meg	Kira	Juan
45	72	56

4. Write a number that is greater than Meg's stickers.
Draw a quick picture to show your work. Write
two sentences to compare the numbers. Use
words or symbols.

5. Write a number that is less than Kira's stickers.
Draw a quick picture to show your work. Write
two sentences to compare the numbers. Use
words or symbols.

Ned uses buttons to make puppets.
He has 38 round buttons.
He has 7 square buttons.

6. Write an addition sentence to show how many
   buttons Ned has in all. Use pictures, words,
   and numbers.

Wendy uses clay to make animals.
Wendy has 6 packs of clay sticks.
Each pack has 10 sticks.
She uses 2 of her packs to make the animals.

7. Write a subtraction sentence to show how many
   clay sticks Wendy has left. Use pictures, words,
   and numbers.

---

8. Wendy gets 18 more sticks of clay.
   Write an addition sentence to show how many
   clay sticks Wendy has now. Use pictures,
   words, and numbers.

1. Use the 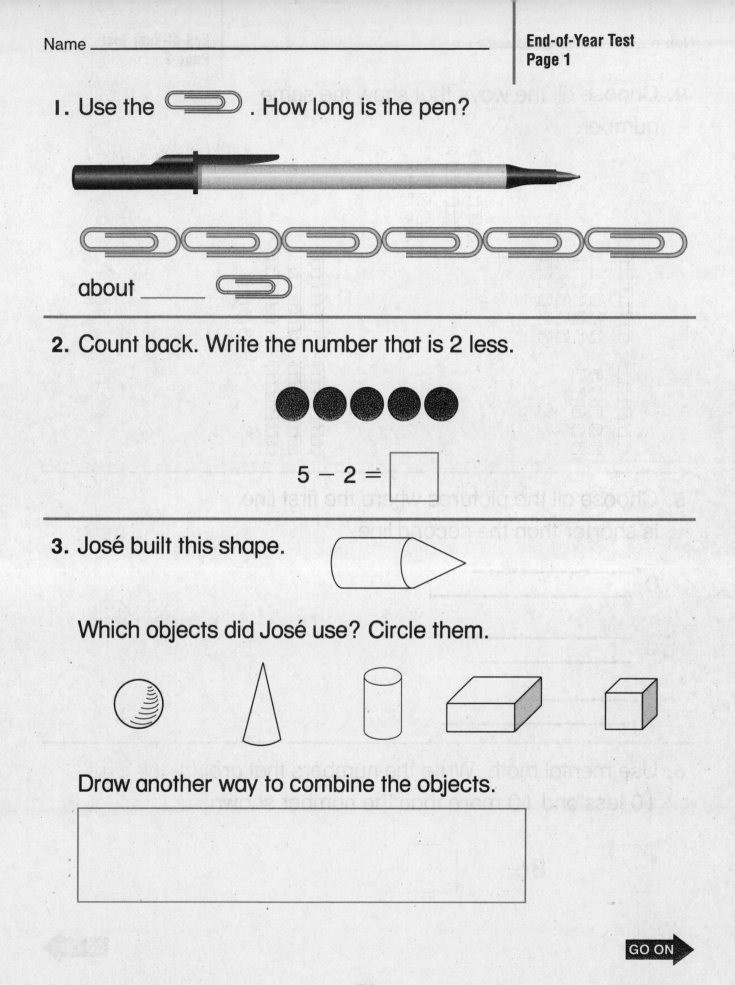 . How long is the pen?

about _____

---

2. Count back. Write the number that is 2 less.

$$5 - 2 = \boxed{}$$

---

3. José built this shape.

Which objects did José use? Circle them.

Draw another way to combine the objects.

GO ON ➡

4. Choose all the ways that show the same
number.

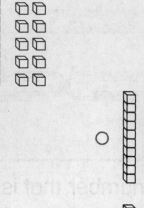

○

○

5. Choose all the pictures where the first line
is shorter than the second line.

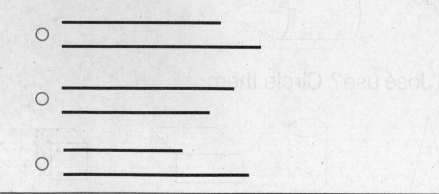

6. Use mental math. Write the numbers that are
10 less and 10 more than the number shown.

86

GO ON ➡

7. Look at the number sentences. What number is missing? Write the number in each box.

$14 - \boxed{} = 8$ $8 + \boxed{} = 14$

---

8. Use the hundred chart to add. Count on by ones or tens.

$37 + 30 =$ _____

Explain how you used the chart to find the sum.

1	2	3	4	5	6	7	8	9	10
11	12	13	14	15	16	17	18	19	20
21	22	23	24	25	26	27	28	29	30
31	32	33	34	35	36	37	38	39	40
41	42	43	44	45	46	47	48	49	50
51	52	53	54	55	56	57	58	59	60
61	62	63	64	65	66	67	68	69	70
71	72	73	74	75	76	77	78	79	80
81	82	83	84	85	86	87	88	89	90
91	92	93	94	95	96	97	98	99	100

---

9. Andy has 12 stickers. He gives 3 away. How many does he have left?

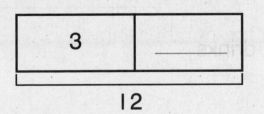

_____ stickers left

GO ON

10. Sid made a pizza.
Color one fourth of the pizza.

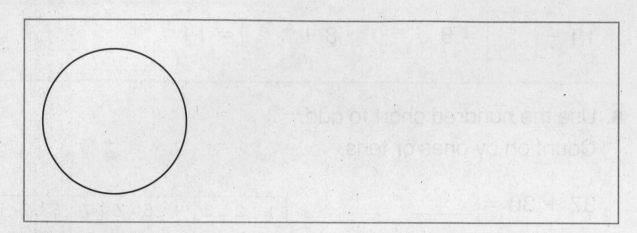

11. Read the problem. Write a number to solve.

I am greater than 65.
I am less than 70.
I have 9 ones.

12. Pippa has 90 drinks in her store.
She sells 80 of them. How many
drinks are left? Show your work.

_____ drinks

End-of-Year Test

13. Choose all the ways that name the time
on the clock.

○ 5:30   ○ 6:30

○ half past 6:00   ○ half past 5:00

---

14. Which shapes have 4 sides?

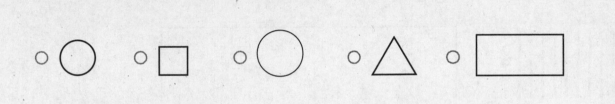

---

15. Write each addition sentence in the box
that shows the sum.

$1 + 7$ $6 + 0$ $3 + 4$ $0 + 6$ $7 + 1$

6	7	8

End-of-Year Test

16. Look at the facts. A number is missing.
Which number is missing?

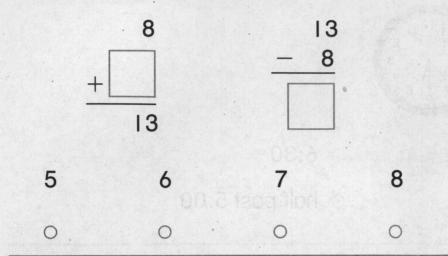

$$8$$
$$+ \boxed{}$$
$$\overline{13}$$

$$13$$
$$- 8$$
$$\boxed{}$$

5	6	7	8
○	○	○	○

17. Finish the drawing to show 100.

Write to explain.

18. Circle the numbers that make the
sentence true.

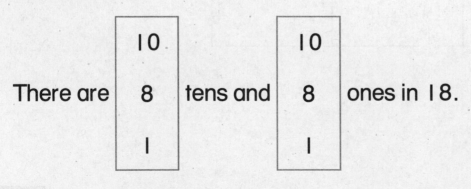

There are [10 / 8 / 1] tens and [10 / 8 / 1] ones in 18.

GO ON

Write a number to make the sentence true.

19. _____ + 7 = 7 + 6

Use the bar graph to answer questions 20 and 21.

20. Compare ◊ and ☼ days. Circle the number that makes the sentence true.

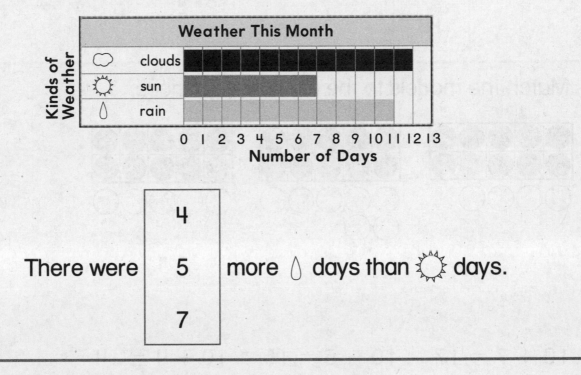

There were | 4 | 5 | 7 | more ◊ days than ☼ days.

---

21. Ann says the graph shows 1 more rainy day than cloudy days. Is she correct? Explain your answer.

22. Circle the number that makes the sentence true. Liam has 6 green marbles, 5 blue marbles, and 7 black marbles. How many marbles does he have in all?

Liam has
| 14 |
| 17 | marbles.
| 18 |

---

23. Match the models to the number sentences.

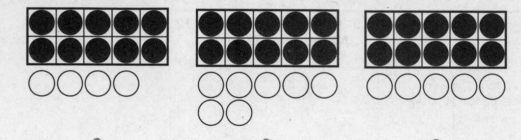

$10 + 7 = 17 \qquad 10 + 5 = 15 \qquad 10 + 4 = 14$

---

24. Marcus has 56 blocks. Tanya has 58 blocks. Compare. Write the numbers that make the sentence true.

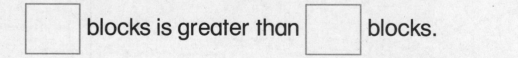

☐ blocks is greater than ☐ blocks.

Max Takes Measurements

**Max is telling time and comparing things.
Help Max take measurements and
record data.**

1. Max draws an hour hand pointing between
   9 and 10 on the clock. Then he draws a
   minute hand on the 6. Draw Max's clock.
   Write the time.

2. Max draws an hour hand pointing to the
   number 3 on the clock. Then he draws a
   minute hand on the 12. Draw Max's clock.
   Write the time.

GO ON

79

Max uses to measure things.
Use .
Draw the things that Max measures.

3. Draw a marker that is about 5 long.

_____

4. Draw a pencil that is longer than the marker.
About how many long is it?

_____

_____

5. Draw a crayon that is shorter than the marker.
About how many long is it?

_____

_____

6. Write the names of the three objects in order
from shortest to longest.

GO ON →

End-of-Year Test

Max asked 18 kids which day they like best: Friday, Saturday, or Sunday. Nine children chose Saturday. Three children chose Sunday. The rest of the children chose Friday.

7. Make a tally chart to show the children's choices.

FAVORITE DAY		Total
Friday		
Saturday		
Sunday		

Now use the tally chart to answer the questions.

8. How many children chose Friday? _____

9. How many more children chose Saturday than Sunday? _____

10. How many children chose Friday and Sunday in all? _____

Fourteen kids in Max's class each have one pet. Max makes a bar graph to show each pet and the number of kids who have it. Seven kids have a dog. Four have a cat. Three have a fish.

11. Complete Max's bar graph.

PETS

Pet										
dog										
cat										
fish										

Number of Children

Now use the graph to answer the questions.

12. Which pet do the most children have? ______

13. Which pet do the least children have? ______

14. How many dogs and fish in all do the children have? ______

15. How many more children have a dog than a cat? ______

STOP

The Fruit Market

Evan and April go to the fruit market.
They each pick out some fruit to share.

April buys 8 apples.
Some are red.
The rest are green.

1. Draw April's apples. Write an addition
   sentence about them.

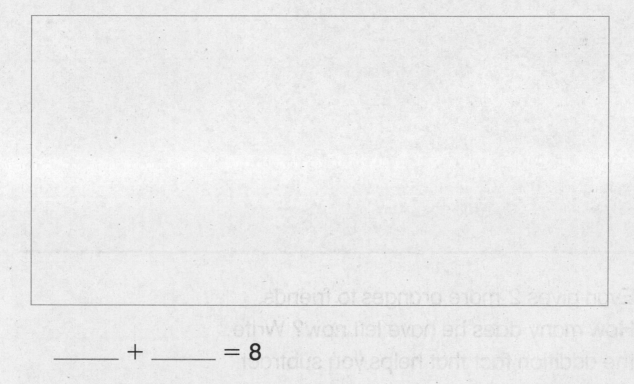

_____ + _____ = 8

---

2. Write a related addition fact about April's apples.

_____ + _____ = _____

3. Evan buys some oranges. He gives 1, 2,
   or 3 oranges to April. He has 5 oranges
   left. Draw pictures and write a number
   sentence to show how many oranges
   Evan could have bought.

4. Evan gives 2 more oranges to friends.
   How many does he have left now? Write
   the addition fact that helps you subtract.

Pablo buys between 11 and 19 peaches.

5. Draw to show a number of peaches
   Pablo could buy. Circle to show tens
   and ones in the drawing.

---

6. Draw to show the number of peaches
   in another way.

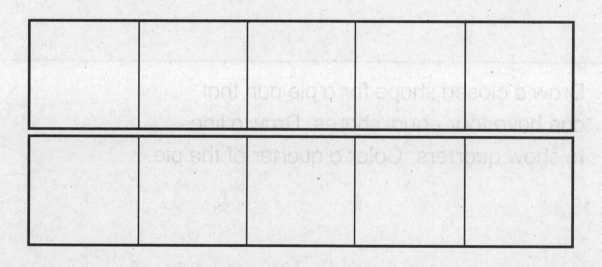

---

7. Write how many tens and ones.

   _____ tens   _____ ones

   Write the number of peaches. _____

© Houghton Mifflin Harcourt Publishing Company

GO ON

**Pablo bakes the peaches into pies
that he can share with friends.**

8. Draw a closed shape for a pie pan that
can have two equal shares. Draw a line
to show halves. Color half of the pie.

9. Draw a closed shape for a pie pan that
can have four equal shares. Draw a line
to show quarters. Color a quarter of the pie.